Panoramic
AUSTRALIA

Panoramic
AUSTRALIA

First published in 1996 by
New Holland (Publishers) Ltd
London • Cape Town • Sydney • Singapore

Produced in Australia by
New Holland Publishers
3/2 Aquatic Drive, Frenchs Forest
NSW 2086, Australia

24 Nutford Place
London W1H 6DQ
United Kingdom

80 McKenzie Street
Cape Town 8001
South Africa

ISBN 1 86436 251 0

CAPTIONS AND EDITING: Anouska Good
DESIGNER: Petal Palmer
DESIGN ASSISTANT: Lellyn Creamer
PUBLISHING MANAGER: Mariëlle Renssen
CONSULTANT: Averill Chase
DTP CARTOGRAPHER: John Loubser

REPRODUCTION: Unifoto (Pty) Ltd
Printed by Times Offset (M) Sdn Bhd

Contents

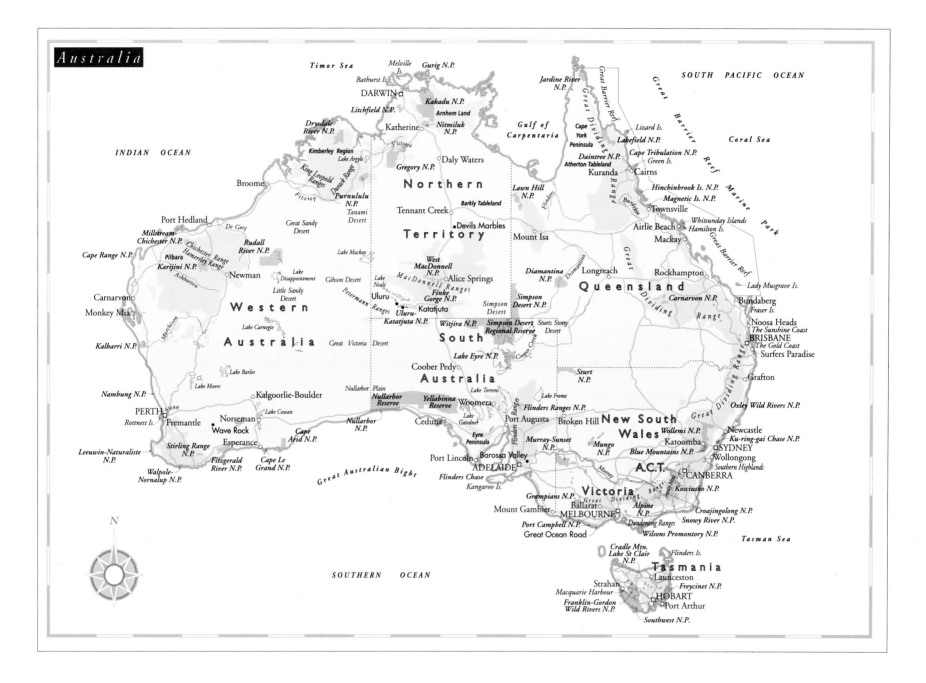

Australia

Timor Sea

SOUTH PACIFIC OCEAN

Melville Is.
Gurig N.P.
Bathurst Is.
Jardine River N.P.

Great Barrier Reef

Great

Coral Sea

DARWIN
Kakadu N.P.
Litchfield N.P.
Arnhem Land
Nitmiluk N.P.
Katherine

Barrier

Lizard Is.
Cape York Peninsula
Lakefield N.P.
Cape Tribulation N.P.
Green Is.

Reef

Gulf of Carpentaria
Cape Dividing Range
Daintree N.P.
Atherton Tableland
Kuranda
Cairns

Marine Park

INDIAN OCEAN

Drysdale River N.P.
Kimberley Region
Lake Argyle
Gregory N.P.
Victoria
Daly Waters

Broome
King Leopold Ranges
Purnululu N.P.
Fitzroy
Tanami Desert

Hinchinbrook Is. N.P.
Magnetic Is. N.P.
Townsville

Northern
Barkly Tableland
Lawn Hill N.P.
Flinders
Airlie Beach
Whitsunday Islands
Hamilton Is.
Mackay

Port Hedland
De Grey
Great Sandy Desert
Tennant Creek
Devils Marbles
Mount Isa
Burdekin

Great Barrier Reef

Millstream-Chichester N.P.
Chichester Range
Rudall River N.P.
Lake Mackay

Territory

Diamantina N.P.
Longreach
Rockhampton
Lady Musgrave Is.

Cape Range N.P.
Pilbara
Hamersley Range
Karijini N.P.
Newman
Ashburton
Lake Disappointment
Gibson Desert
West MacDonnell N.P.
MacDonnell Ranges
Alice Springs
Diamantina

Queensland
Carnarvon N.P.
Bundaberg
Fraser Is.

Carnarvon
Monkey Mia
Little Sandy Desert
Lake Neale
Uluru
Finke Gorge N.P.
Katatjuta
Simpson Desert
Simpson Desert N.P.

Great Dividing Range

Noosa Heads
The Sunshine Coast
BRISBANE

Kalbarri N.P.
Western
Lake Carnegie
Petermann Ranges
Uluru-Katatjuta N.P.
Witjira N.P.
Simpson Desert Regional Reserve
Sturts Stony Desert

The Gold Coast
Surfers Paradise

Australia
South

Grafton

Nambung N.P.
Lake Barlee
Lake Moore
Great Victoria Desert
Australia
Lake Eyre N.P.
Cooper Creek
Sturt N.P.

Coober Pedy

PERTH
Kalgoorlie-Boulder
Nullarbor Plain
Nullarbor Reserve
Yellabinna Reserve
Woomera
Lake Torrens
Lake Frome
Flinders Ranges N.P.
Oxley Wild Rivers N.P.

New South Wales
Wollemi N.P.
Newcastle
Ku-ring-gai Chase N.P.
Katoomba
SYDNEY

Rottnest Is.
Fremantle
Norseman
Wave Rock
Lake Cowan
Nullarbor N.P.
Ceduna
Lake Gairdner
Port Augusta
Broken Hill
Mungo N.P.
Blue Mountains N.P.
Wollongong

Leeuwin-Naturaliste N.P.
Stirling Range N.P.
Esperance
Cape Arid N.P.
Eyre Peninsula
Port Lincoln
Murray-Sunset N.P.
Murray
A.C.T.
CANBERRA
Southern Highlands
Kosciusko N.P.

Walpole-Nornalup N.P.
Fitzgerald River N.P.
Cape Le Grand N.P.
Great Australian Bight
Flinders Chase
Kangaroo Is.
Barossa Valley
ADELAIDE
Snowy River
Croajingolong N.P.

Victoria
Grampians N.P.
Ballarat
MELBOURNE
Alpine N.P.
Snowy River N.P.
Great Dividing Range
Dandenong Ranges

Mount Gambier
Port Campbell N.P.
Great Ocean Road
Wilsons Promontory N.P.

Tasman Sea

Cradle Mtn.
Lake St Clair N.P.
Flinders Is.

Tasmania
Launceston
Freycinet N.P.

SOUTHERN OCEAN

Strahan
Macquarie Harbour
Franklin-Gordon Wild Rivers N.P.
HOBART
Port Arthur

Southwest N.P.

N

OPPOSITE, TOP LEFT Dawn breaks over the beautiful city of Sydney. It is hard to believe that this vibrant and cosmopolitan city had its roots in a penal colony, the Union Jack having been raised on the shores of Sydney Cove (today's Circular Quay) in 1788.

OPPOSITE, TOP RIGHT Glebe Island Bridge is Sydney's newest landmark and was only opened for use in 1995.

LEFT Sydney Harbour Bridge is one of the largest single-span bridges in the world. Completed in 1932, it provides the link between the northern and southern sides of the harbour.

BELOW The Opera House and the Harbour Bridge, situated at the centre of the city, are separated by Circular Quay, from where ferries leave for many harbour destinations. With its dramatic white sails, designed to echo those of the yachts in the harbour, the Opera House has become Sydney's most distinctive symbol.

ABOVE Yachts moored at Cremorne Point on the northern side of the harbour. Cremorne is also one of the stops for the ferries that cross Sydney Harbour.

LEFT The Sydney Opera House has five performance halls offering visitors a range of activities including ballet, opera and drama. Adjacent to the Opera House are the lush grounds of the Botanic Gardens which date back to 1816.

ABOVE, LEFT TO RIGHT The Rocks, today a complex of pubs, restaurants and shops aimed mainly at tourists, is the oldest area of the city.

ABOVE The Rocks began life more than 200 years ago and for a time was the centre of Sydney's wild military and convict nightlife.

ABOVE Many of the old warehouses and buildings have now been restored and converted into eateries and fascinating galleries.

ABOVE The gardens of Government House, dating back to the 1840s, are open to the public seven days a week. Tours of the house itself are also possible.

ABOVE From Observatory Hill, the site of the old Sydney Observatory from 1858 to 1982, it is possible to enjoy spectacular views of The Rocks with the Harbour Bridge dominating the skyline. Visitors can still book night-sky viewings at the Observatory, which is now a museum of astronomy.

ABOVE AND LEFT Darling Harbour offers gift shops, restaurants and conference facilities. The Chinese Gardens are a favourite on weekends.

ABOVE Open-air markets, an amusement park and the National Maritime Museum are among the attractions that bring people flocking to the complex.

PREVIOUS PAGES A view over Sydney Harbour from Kirribilli. This harbour-side suburb is where the official Sydney residences of Australia's Governor-General and Prime Minister are to be found.

BELOW RIGHT Kings Cross, initially an upmarket residential area, is today known for its colourful night life and backpacker hostels.

ABOVE, TOP LEFT AND RIGHT, AND BOTTOM LEFT The Queen Victoria Building, with its copper domes and cupolas, occupies an entire city block.
OPPOSITE A view of the city from Darling Harbour, dominated by the Sydney Tower which soars above the Centrepoint complex.

THIS PAGE Two of the best ferry trips across the harbour are to Taronga Zoo and Manly. Taronga, voted best international zoo in 1992, houses an impressive collection of Australian wildlife. Manly offers everything the daytripper could want, from great beaches to outdoor restaurants and buskers.

PREVIOUS PAGES One of the best-known restaurants in Australia is Doyle's at Watsons Bay. Enjoying delicious seafood while overlooking the sparkling waters of the bay is an experience not to be missed.

ABOVE The cliffs and headlands adjacent to many of Sydney's beaches are popular spots for adventurous hang-gliders.

ABOVE Bondi's lifesavers are renowned for their skill, and are often called into service during the summer surf carnivals.

RIGHT Crowds flock to Bondi Beach during the summer months.

ABOVE Barrenjoey Lighthouse, overlooking the entrance to Broken Bay, stands at Palm Beach, the most northerly of the beachside suburbs.

LEFT Curl Curl is one of Sydney's northern beaches and forms part of a series of beautiful white sand beaches extending up the coast.

ABOVE AND OPPOSITE The Ku-ring-gai Chase National Park, a haven for bush-walking and birdwatching, lies 30km north of Sydney. The many waterways which weave through the parkland are ideal for houseboats and waterskiers.

ABOVE The Blue Mountains are a series of deeply weathered sandstone canyons clothed with lush eucalypt forest. With spectacular views across the Jamison and Megalong valleys, the area around Katoomba is a major tourist attraction.

LEFT The Three Sisters rock formation is best viewed from Echo Point. Aboriginal legend has it that the sisters were turned to stone by their father to protect them from the wicked bunyip (an imaginary creature) in the valley below.

ABOVE Kosciusko National Park is situated in the Snowy Mountains and is home to Mt Kosciusko, at 2228m Australia's highest peak.

ABOVE Australia is known for the astonishing variety of its indigenous wildlife. The common ringtail possum, seen here with its young, is one of the less visible species.

ABOVE, LEFT AND RIGHT Towns such as Bowral and Berry are reminiscent of old England with their lush rolling farmland and quaint guesthouses.

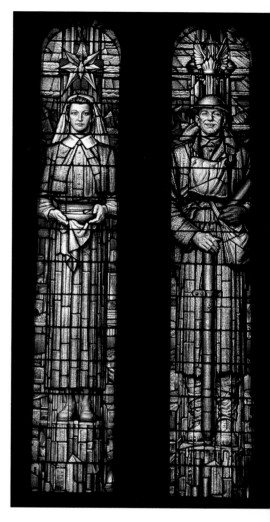

ABOVE The National War Memorial, opened in 1941, houses a huge collection of relics and paintings recalling all the wars in which Australia has been involved. The walls of the cloisters are lined with Honour Rolls for each conflict, remembering the many members of the armed services who gave their lives for Australia.

ABOVE RIGHT Stained-glass windows inspire awe in the National War Memorial's Hall of Memory, the resting place for the tomb of Australia's Unknown Soldier.

LEFT New Parliament House on Capital Hill in Canberra, Australia's capital city, is the place to see Australian democracy in action. The unique grass roof is designed to recreate the hill which was excavated to make way for the new building.

ABOVE Brisbane's riverside development overlooking the Eagle Street Pier offers a variety of excellent cafes and restaurants.

PREVIOUS PAGES Brisbane is the capital of Queensland, also known as the 'Sunshine State', and has at its heart the gently flowing waters of the Brisbane River.

ABOVE Story Bridge, designed by JC Bradfield (the designer of the Sydney Harbour Bridge), is the most famous of the seven bridges that cross the Brisbane River.

FOLLOWING PAGES Queensland's Gold Coast is home to beautiful beaches, high-rise apartment blocks, luxurious hotels, and theme parks such as Sea World.

ABOVE The Big Pineapple, golden and gleaming beside the Bruce Highway, captures the spirit of the Sunshine Coast.

RIGHT The Sunshine Coast's hinterland is a rich agricultural region. Dairy farming is the dominant industry in the area.

PREVIOUS PAGES Surfers Paradise is the centre of the Gold Coast.

ABOVE Queensland's long hot summers attract sun lovers from all over the world. Here, outrigger-canoeing competitors head through the surf at Noosa Heads.

LEFT Situated on the northern stretch of the Sunshine Coast, upmarket Noosa Heads has a number of exclusive resorts.

ABOVE Sugarcane, grown in the Bundaberg area since 1866, is used in the popular Bundaberg rum.

LEFT AND RIGHT Fraser Island, the largest sand island in the world, bewitches with its quiet streams, sand-dune lakes, rugged headlands, and soaring cliffs. Dingoes are sometimes seen on the beaches.

BELOW Hamilton Island, one of the most luxurious resort destinations along the Great Barrier Reef, is the playground of the wealthy.

FOLLOWING PAGES The Great Barrier Reef, the largest living organism on the planet, stretches for over 2000km along the Queensland coast.

ABOVE The crystal-clear waters around Lady Musgrave Island are a paradise for snorkellers and scuba divers.

ABOVE The glass-bottomed 'Yellow Submarine' enables nonswimmers to view the reefs around Green Island.

RIGHT Airlie Beach is near Shute Harbour, the gateway to the glorious Whitsunday Islands.

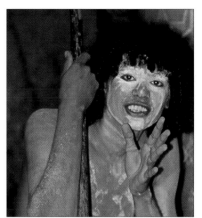

OPPOSITE, TOP LEFT Daintree River National Park is a rainforest wilderness with Mossman Gorge as one of the few easily accessible areas.

OPPOSITE, TOP RIGHT Aboriginal culture includes ceremonies that fuse song, dance and body painting. The Tjapukai Dance Theatre enables visitors to gain some understanding of this rich art form.

LEFT One of the most scenic ways to view the rainforest is to take the train from Cairns to the picturesque station at Kuranda.

BELOW Australia's rainforests are home to thousands of plant species, many of which are still to be discovered or fully understood.

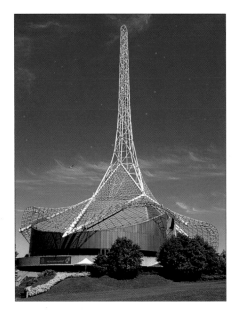

ABOVE LEFT AND RIGHT, AND BELOW   Melbourne, Victoria's capital, is famous for its Arts Centre, outdoor sculptures, historic buildings and trams.

RIGHT   The city sprawls along the banks of the Yarra River. The imposing Princes Bridge connects one of Melbourne's main arteries, St Kilda Road, to the Central Business District.

PREVIOUS PAGES   Established in 1835, Melbourne is Australia's second-largest city and home to over 3 million people.

ABOVE The multicultural nature of Melbourne, with its large Greek and Italian communities, is evident in the names of the delicatessens and restaurants along Lygon Street in Carlton.

LEFT While Melbourne's skyline is dominated by recently built high-rise complexes, splendid late-19th-century buildings remain. St Paul's Cathedral is a fine example of Gothic Revival architecture.

ABOVE AND RIGHT The Twelve Apostles in Port Campbell National Park were once part of the mainland. Over time, the stone pillars separated due to the erosive forces of the elements.

ABOVE Puffing Billy is one of the Dandenongs' most popular attractions. The locomotive that pulls the train was designed at the turn of the century for the narrow-gauge tracks.

LEFT Loch Ard Gorge, seen from the Great Ocean Road, is the site of one of the most tragic shipwrecks occurring on this rugged coast. During the last century, the clipper *Loch Ard* smashed onto the rocks; only two passengers survived the ordeal.

ABOVE AND RIGHT The Grampians, part of the Great Dividing Range, boast spectacular rock formations such as the Balconies (pictured) and the beautiful McKenzie Falls.

ABOVE The township of Sovereign Hill, near Ballarat, recreates the days of Australia's 19th-century gold rushes.

ABOVE Dressed in authentic uniforms, these 'officers' form part of the Sovereign Hill experience.

ABOVE Each of Australia's states has its own breweries and Tasmania is no exception. The beer produced at Cascade Brewery is widely held to be among the best.

LEFT Constitution Dock, which once a year sees the arrival of the ocean-going yachts in the Sydney to Hobart race, is normally home to fishing trawlers.

PREVIOUS PAGES The smallest of Australia's states, Tasmania is an area of immense natural beauty. From Mount Wellington it is possible to look out over the capital, Hobart, and the spectacular Derwent River.

ABOVE LEFT AND RIGHT, AND BELOW Every weekend Tasmanians and tourists flock to the popular Salamanca Markets. There is entertainment for everyone and many bargains to be had.

RIGHT The Georgian warehouses of Salamanca Place have been painstakingly converted into restaurants, gift shops and galleries.

LEFT Situated on the Tasman Peninsula are the ruins of the notorious penal colony, Port Arthur. Thousands of convicts entered its forbidding walls during the 47 years of its existence and nearly 2000 were buried on the nearby Isle of the Dead.

OPPOSITE, TOP RIGHT The historic church at Port Arthur is without a roof or windows and stands on a hill overlooking the prison.

OPPOSITE, TOP LEFT AND BELOW Port Arthur aimed to be self-sufficient and convicts were employed in such diverse industries as ship-building and clothing manufacture. The flour mill (pictured) was converted into cells, however.

ABOVE Strahan is a small, picturesque fishing town located on the edge of breathtaking Macquarie Harbour, one of the largest natural harbours in Australia.

RIGHT Much of western Tasmania is rugged and mountainous with lush vegetation, plunging gorges and jagged peaks. The sheer cliffs of Frenchmans Cap dominate the surrounding landscape.

ABOVE The Tasmanian devil was given its name by the early settlers because of its ferocious appearance; however, the devil is actually a shy creature and almost entirely nocturnal.

ABOVE AND LEFT Freycinet National Park is noted for its spectacular coastal scenery and is a favourite destination for bushwalkers and climbers.

ABOVE RIGHT Wallabies are endemic to Australia and New Guinea as these once formed part of the same landmass; several different species occur.

TOP LEFT, ABOVE AND RIGHT The wild green slopes of Cradle Mountain change dramatically in winter when storms lash Lake Dove and snow covers the landscape.

ABOVE The impressive Festival Centre on the banks of the Torrens Lake is the venue for the biennial Adelaide Arts Festival.

ABOVE AND RIGHT The elegant capital of South Australia, Adelaide is situated on the banks of the River Torrens.

ABOVE AND LEFT The city is a gracious blend of old and new with historic buildings contrasting with modern hotels.

ABOVE Often referred to as the 'City of Churches', Adelaide's skyline is dotted with numerous spires.

LEFT Kangaroos hop freely around the island of the same name; Kangaroo Island is also home to hundreds of birds and other animals including wallabies, possums, koalas, snakes and seals. Picnic and camping facilities are available allowing visitors to take advantage of the spectacular scenery.

OPPOSITE TOP A short drive from Kingscote, the Cygnet Cafe on Kangaroo Island's north coast is renowned for its spread of local produce.

BELOW Kangaroo Island is Australia's third-largest island and contains South Australia's largest national park, Flinders Chase. The coastline changes from tranquil beaches in the north to rugged cliffs in the south.

ABOVE AND BELOW The Remarkable Rocks, at Kirkpatrick Point on Kangaroo Island, have been sculpted over time into strange shapes by the wind and sea.

LEFT The mighty cliffs, which plunge more than 90m into the cold waters of the Great Australian Bight, mark the end of the vast Nullarbor Plain.

ABOVE AND BELOW The Barossa Valley, Australia's famous wine-producing region, is also home to many beautiful old homesteads such as Elderton (above) and Collingrove (below).

RIGHT Within the Barossa Valley, conditions vary considerably enabling a wide range of wines to be produced.

ABOVE, LEFT AND RIGHT Everything at Coober Pedy, from the 'Opal Cave' tourist complex to the church, is built underground in order to escape the blazing heat. In summer, temperatures can soar as high as 54°C; during winter, however, the nights are freezing.

ABOVE Situated in the heart of Australia's outback, the mining town of Coober Pedy sprang to life when opals were discovered here in 1911.

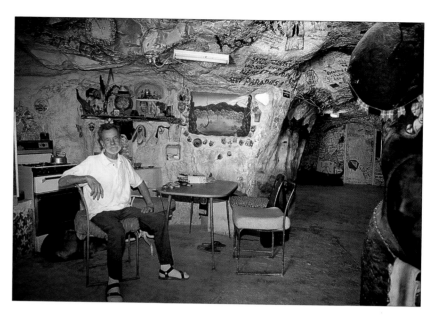

ABOVE LEFT The town, aware of its unique lifestyle, caters for tourists and the underground bookshop provides visitors with all the information they could ever need. It also enables them to experience life underground, even if only for a short while.

TOP RIGHT AND ABOVE, LEFT AND RIGHT Occupied by interesting characters, the homes at Coober Pedy are comfortably equipped and carefully decorated.

ABOVE AND BELOW The charming old port of
Fremantle is known for its colonial heritage.

RIGHT Western Australia is known as the 'Wildflower State' and blossoms every
spring with a seemingly endless carpet of different species and colours.

PREVIOUS PAGES Kings Park, on top of Mount Eliza, offers superb views of
Western Australia's capital Perth and the blue waters of the Swan River.

ABOVE A replica of Captain James Cook's ship, the *Endeavour*, sets sail from Fremantle.

ABOVE The Esplanade Hotel, Fremantle.
RIGHT The bustling town of Fremantle today has virtually become a suburb of Perth.

ABOVE The quokka, a tiny marsupial which is found principally on Rottnest Island, was initially believed by early settlers to be a kind of rat.

ABOVE AND LEFT Rottnest Island is both a wildlife reserve and Perth's premier holiday destination, offering magnificent scenery and complete relaxation. As there are no cars on the island, bicycles are the popular form of transport.

ABOVE AND BELOW The south-west is the state's agricultural heartland. Sheep grazing, wheat farming and vegetable growing all contribute to the region's economy.

RIGHT Wave Rock, situated over 350km inland from Perth near the township of Hyden, is a 15m-high granite rock that has been sculpted over the years by wind erosion.

ABOVE AND LEFT Rising from the sands of the Nambung National Park, the Pinnacles are one of Western Australia's most unusual landforms.

ABOVE Thought to have formed along the roots of ancient desert plants, these limestone pillars cast enigmatic shadows across the dunes.

ABOVE, BELOW LEFT AND CENTRE Kalbarri National Park north of Geraldton is famed for its over 500 species of wildflower and its dramatic coastal gorges. The park is home to a variety of wildlife, including emus.

ABOVE RIGHT Monkey Mia, at Shark Bay in Western Australia's Gascoyne region, is famous for its dolphins. In 1964, a woman from one of the fishing camps handfed one of the dolphins, thus beginning a tradition of handfeeding which continues to this day.

ABOVE The spectacular cliffs at Loop Bend in the Kalbarri National Park provide tourists with an opportunity to survey the beauty of the region.

ABOVE AND RIGHT The Bungle Bungles, known to the Aborigines as Purnululu, were formed over 350 million years ago. Horizontal bands in the sandstone are covered by thin layers of black lichens and orange silica.

PREVIOUS PAGES The quaint mining town of Kalgoorlie became the heart of the West Australian gold fields when Paddy Hannan discovered the first gold there in 1893. Some fine examples of early Australian architecture have been preserved, including the Metropole Hotel.

ABOVE Alice Springs, located virtually in the centre of Australia, is a thriving town first established when the Overland Telegraph was being built in the 1870s.

ABOVE AND LEFT Katatjuta, previously known as the Olgas, is named after the Aboriginal word for 'many heads'. The sandstone formation is a sacred Aborginal site.

PREVIOUS PAGES Uluru, formerly Ayers Rock, is a sandstone monolith that rises 348m above the surrounding landscape. Uluru's mystical quality is enhanced by the way it changes colour as the day progresses.

ABOVE AND RIGHT The Devils Marbles are a cluster of red granite rocks to the south of Tennant Creek. Aboriginal legend has it that they are the eggs of the Rainbow Serpent.

FOLLOWING PAGES At Kakadu National Park visitors are taken on cruises through the wetlands where they have a chance to spot estuarine crocodiles, among other wildlife.

Above, left and right   At Nourlangie Rock in Kakadu National Park there are many examples of traditional Aboriginal rock art.

Above left   The people who inhabit Australia's 'Red Centre' have learnt over the centuries how to survive in the unforgiving outback landscape.
Above centre   Didgeridoos traditionally provide the musical accompaniment at Aboriginal tribal ceremonies such as corroborees.
Above right and opposite   These magnetic termite mounds in Litchfield National Park, so-called because they always face north-south, are formed from mud digested by the thousands of termites that inhabit them.

ABOVE To the south of Darwin, the beautiful Florence Falls are among the most striking waterfalls that tumble across the escarpment.

ABOVE Darwin, the capital of the Northern Territory, is a cosmopolitan city with superb beaches and a tropical climate. As a result, it is becoming an increasingly popular tourist destination. The harbour is twice the size of Sydney Harbour.

ABOVE Parliament House was built after Cyclone Tracey devastated the city on Christmas Eve in 1974.
ABOVE RIGHT AND BELOW LEFT The Botanical Gardens, spread over 34ha, are one of Darwin's main attractions.

ABOVE RIGHT As well as a variety of eateries, the Wharf Precinct offers a number of interesting tours, exhibitions and week-end entertainment. Dolphins are often seen around the wharf in the evenings.
LEFT Darwin's Government House, first constructed in 1872, was pulled down and rebuilt in the 1880s.

ABOVE LEFT AND RIGHT Bronco riding and steer wrestling challenge the courage and skills of the local 'cowboys' at a Darwin rodeo.

ABOVE Rodeos are an extremely popular form of entertainment in the Territory and attract hundreds of residents and visitors alike.